DIABETIC
Cooking
FOR 1 OR 2

Publications International, Ltd.

Favorite Brand Name Recipes at www.fbnr.com

Recipe Development: Cheryl Chrysler and Elizabeth Matlin, FoodWorks®;
Donna Shields; Marcia Kay Stanley, M.S., R.D.

Nutritional Analysis: Linda R. Yoakam, M.S., R.D., L.D.

Photography on pages 7, 11, 19, 21, 25, 29, 41, 49, 51, 53, 57, 61, 63, 67, 69, 75, 79, 81 and 83 by Laurie Proffitt Photography, Chicago.

Photography on pages 13, 15, 31, 33, 37, 39, 45, 47, 71, 77, 87 and 91 by Audrey Nilsen Photography.

Pictured on the front cover *(clockwise from top left)*: Jamaican Jerk Turkey Wraps *(page 50)*, Vegetable & Tofu Gratin *(page 70)*, Spicy Black Bean & Sausage Stew *(page 14)* and Easy Citrus Berry Shortcake *(page 86)*.

Pictured on the back cover: Baked Pear Dessert *(page 80)*

ISBN: 0-7853-4010-6

Manufactured in U.S.A.

8 7 6 5 4 3 2 1

Microwave Cooking: Microwave ovens vary in wattage. Use the cooking times as guidelines and check for doneness before adding more time.

DIABETIC Cooking FOR 1 OR 2

Cooking for One or Two

Cooking for just yourself or yourself and one other person has many challenges. Most recipes make 4 or more servings. That means you may be tempted to eat more than one serving. Or, you must deal with leftovers tomorrow. Sometimes it just seems easier to buy a frozen meal, carry-out food or even fast food. For people with diabetes every meal is important and the challenge to make it a healthy one is always present. *Diabetic Cooking for 1 or 2* is the perfect solution to these problems.

In the **"Dinner for One or Two"** chapter, you'll find a delightful assortment of recipes, some for just one and many for two. All of the recipes are suitable for everyday meals. From pasta dishes to casseroles and stir-fries, you'll find lots of choices. These recipes can easily be doubled for those occasions when you need to serve more.

The **"5 Ingredients or Less"** chapter was designed for those who don't have much time to spend cooking or those looking for extra-easy meals. Not included in the five ingredients are salt, pepper, water, cooking oil or nonstick cooking spray—items you have on hand. You'll be amazed just how delicious five ingredients can be.

"Two-for-One Dinners" offers you a new twist on leftovers. Prepare the first recipe and save a portion of it to use to make a second recipe another day. Wow! Leftovers that don't look or taste like leftovers. The second day recipes have the added bonus of being quick to fix.

"Meatless Dinners" offers you the choice of a lower-protein meal. These recipes are also suitable for a dinner guest who is vegetarian. If you need more protein, simply add two or three ounces of lean chicken, turkey, fish or meat.

When a sugar-free packaged cookie just won't do, choose a fabulously easy dessert from **"Delicious Desserts."** Some have no sugar added and others use small amounts of sugar. Carbohydrate contents range from 15 to 37 grams.

Cooking Equipment

Most of the recipes in this publication require skillets and saucepans that you use every day. Some of the recipes require small casseroles or baking dishes (1½ cups to 1½ quarts). If you don't have these, look for inexpensive 4-cup and 6-cup ovenproof, microwavable storage containers (available at supermarkets or mass merchandisers). Large custard cups, individual soufflé dishes, and 7×5-inch baking dishes and small gratin dishes are also excellent choices. A great source for small casseroles, soufflé and gratin dishes is garage or yard sales. Unless they are marked as microwave-safe, use these casseroles only in a conventional oven. A small scale can be a useful, but not necessary, tool for measuring fruits, vegetables, meat and small amounts of pasta.

Keep this book handy and you'll be just minutes away from a delicious meal.

7

About the Recipes

The recipes in *Diabetic Cooking for 1 or 2* were specifically developed for people with diabetes. All are based on the principals of sound nutrition as outlined by the dietary guidelines developed by the United States Department of Agriculture and the United States Department of Health and Human Services, making them perfect for the entire family.

Although the recipes are not intended as a medically therapeutic program, nor as a substitute for medically approved meal plans for individuals with diabetes, they contain amounts of calories, fat, cholesterol, sodium and carbohydrate that will fit easily into an individualized meal plan designed by your physician, certified diabetes educator or registered dietitian, and you.

The goal of this publication is to provide a variety of recipe choices for people with diabetes. Since diabetic meal plans can vary a great deal from one individual to another, not all recipes may be suitable for every person with diabetes. Therefore, each individual must choose wisely from among the recipes in this book based on information provided by their physician, certified diabetes educator or registered dietitian, and their past experience.

A Few Words about Sugar

In 1994, the American Diabetes Association lifted the absolute ban on sugar from the recommended dietary guidelines for people with diabetes. Under updated guidelines, you can, for example, exchange 1 tablespoon of sugar for a slice of bread because each is considered a starch exchange. The new guidelines for sugar intake are based on scientific studies that show that carbohydrate in the form of sugars does not raise blood glucose levels any more rapidly than other types of carbohydrate-containing food. What is more important is the total amount of carbohydrate eaten, not the source.

However, keep in mind that sweets and other foods high in sugar are usually high in calories and fat and contain few, if any, other nutrients, so the choice between an apple and a doughnut is still an easy one to make. Nobody, diabetic or not, should be eating foods filled with lots of sugar. But, when calculated into the nutritional analysis, a small amount of sugar can enhance a recipe and will not be harmful.

If you have any questions or concerns about incorporating sugar into your daily meal plans, consult your physician and certified diabetes educator or registered dietitian for more information.

Nutritional Analysis

The nutritional analysis that appears with each recipe was calculated by an independent nutritional consulting firm. Every effort has been made to check the accuracy of these numbers. However, because numerous variables account for a wide range of values in certain foods, all analyses that appear in this publication should be considered approximate.

• The analysis of each recipe includes all the ingredients that are listed in that recipe, except those labeled as "optional." Nutritional analysis is provided for the primary recipe only, not the recipe variations.

• If a range of amounts is offered for an ingredient (1 to 1¼ cups), the first amount given was used to calculate the nutritional information.

• If an ingredient is presented with an option ("1 cup hot cooked rice or noodles" for example), the first item listed was used to calculate the nutritional information.

• Foods shown in photographs on the same serving plate or offered as "serving suggestions" at the end of the recipe are not included in the recipe analysis unless they are listed in the ingredient list.

• In recipes calling for cooked rice or pasta or calling for rice or pasta to be cooked according to package directions, the analysis was based on preparation without salt and fat.

Symbols

We have included symbols to help you find those recipes that are especially low in fat, carbohydrate, sodium and sugar, and high in fiber. A symbol also appears with the quick-to-fix recipes.

Low-Fat Recipe
Contains 3 grams or less of fat per serving

Low-Carbohydrate Recipe
Contains 10 grams or less of carbohydrate per serving

Low-Sodium Recipe
Contains 140 milligrams or less of sodium per serving

No-Sugar-Added Recipe
Contains no added sugar (granulated, brown or powdered sugar; honey; or corn syrup)

High-Fiber Recipe
Contains 5 grams or more of fiber per serving

20 Minutes or Less
Recipe can be prepared in 20 minutes or less

Dinner for One or Two

20 minutes or less

Plain or fancy—you will find the perfect recipe here.

Seafood & Vegetable Stir-Fry

2 teaspoons olive oil
½ medium red bell pepper, cut into strips
½ medium onion, cut into small wedges
10 snow peas, trimmed and cut into halves
1 clove garlic, minced
6 ounces frozen cooked medium shrimp, thawed
2 tablespoons stir-fry sauce
1 cup hot cooked rice

1. Heat oil in large nonstick skillet over medium-high heat. Add vegetables; stir-fry 4 minutes. Add garlic; stir-fry 1 minute or until vegetables are crisp-tender.

2. Add shrimp and stir-fry sauce. Stir-fry just until hot. Serve over rice. *Makes 2 servings*

Recipe Tip: You may substitute ½ cup thawed frozen snow peas for the fresh ones. Add them in step 1 during the last 2 minutes of stir-frying.

Nutrients per Serving: Calories: 279, Calories from Fat: 19%, Total Fat: 6 g, Saturated Fat: 1 g, Protein: 22 g, Carbohydrate: 33 g, Cholesterol: 166 mg, Sodium: 724 mg, Dietary Fiber: 2 g

Dietary Exchanges: 2 Vegetable, 1½ Starch, 2 Lean Meat

Chicken & Orzo Soup

Nonstick olive oil cooking spray
3 ounces boneless skinless chicken breast, cut into bite-size pieces
1 can (about 14 ounces) fat-free, reduced-sodium chicken broth
1 cup water
⅔ cup shredded carrot
⅓ cup sliced green onion
¼ cup uncooked orzo pasta
1 teaspoon grated fresh ginger
⅛ teaspoon ground turmeric
2 teaspoons lemon juice
Black pepper

1. Spray medium saucepan with cooking spray. Heat over medium-high heat. Add chicken. Cook and stir 2 to 3 minutes or until no longer pink. Remove from saucepan and set aside.

2. In same saucepan combine broth, water, carrot, onion, orzo, ginger and turmeric. Bring to a boil. Reduce heat and simmer, covered, 8 to 10 minutes or until orzo is tender. Stir in chicken and lemon juice; cook until hot. Season to taste with pepper.

3. Ladle into serving bowls. Sprinkle with green onions, if desired.   *Makes 2 servings*

Nutrients per Serving: *Calories: 176, Calories from Fat: 8%, Total Fat: 2 g, Saturated Fat: <1 g, Protein: 18 g, Carbohydrate: 21 g, Cholesterol: 26 mg, Sodium: 182 mg, Dietary Fiber: 2 g*

Dietary Exchanges: *1 Vegetable, 1 Starch, 1½ Lean Meat*

Recipe Tip

Orzo is a tiny rice-shaped pasta. If it is not available, substitute any very small pasta.

12

1 tablespoon olive
 oil
½ cup chopped
 onion
¼ cup chopped
 green bell
 pepper
4 ounces low-fat
 smoked
 sausage, cut
 into ¼-inch
 pieces
2 cloves garlic,
 minced
1 cup drained
 canned black
 beans, rinsed
¾ cup undrained
 no-salt-added
 stewed
 tomatoes
1½ teaspoons dried
 oregano leaves
¾ teaspoon ground
 cumin
2 tablespoons
 minced fresh
 parsley
 Hot pepper sauce,
 to taste

Spicy Black Bean & Sausage Stew

1. Heat oil in medium skillet over medium heat. Add onion, bell pepper and sausage. Cook and stir 3 to 4 minutes or until vegetables are tender. Add garlic; cook and stir 1 minute.

2. Stir in beans, tomatoes, oregano and cumin, breaking up tomatoes into small chunks with spoon. Bring to a boil; reduce heat to low. Cover and simmer 20 minutes, stirring occasionally. Stir in parsley and pepper sauce.　　　*Makes 2 servings*

Serving Suggestion: Top each serving with a mound of ¼ cup hot cooked rice, if desired. This will add 67 calories and 14 grams carbohydrate to each serving.

Nutrients per Serving: *Calories: 266, Calories from Fat: 30%, Total Fat: 11 g, Saturated Fat: 2 g, Protein: 16 g, Carbohydrate: 39 g, Cholesterol: 26 mg, Sodium: 1022 mg, Dietary Fiber: 10 g*

Dietary Exchanges: *1 Vegetable, 2 Starch, 2 Fat*

Recipe Tip

High fiber foods make you feel fuller and are a great way to control hunger. They may also lower total cholesterol and low density lipoprotein (LDL). LDL is often referred to as "bad" cholesterol.

Baked Orange Roughy with Sautéed Vegetables

2 orange roughy fillets (about 4 ounces each)
2 teaspoons olive oil
1 medium carrot, cut into matchstick pieces
4 medium mushrooms, sliced
⅓ cup chopped onion
¼ cup chopped green or yellow bell pepper
1 clove garlic, minced
Black pepper
Lemon wedges

1. Preheat oven to 350°F. Place fish fillets in shallow baking dish. Bake 15 minutes or until fish flakes easily when tested with fork.

2. Heat olive oil in small nonstick skillet over medium-high heat. Add carrots; cook 3 minutes, stirring occasionally. Add mushrooms, onion, bell pepper and garlic; cook and stir 2 minutes or until vegetables are crisp-tender.

3. Place fish on serving plates; top with vegetable mixture. Sprinkle with black pepper. Serve with lemon wedges. *Makes 1 serving*

Notes: To microwave fish, place fish in shallow microwavable dish. Microwave, covered, on HIGH 2 minutes or until fish flakes easily when tested with fork. To broil fish, place fish on rack of broiler pan. Broil 4 to 6 inches from heat 4 minutes on each side or until fish flakes easily when tested with fork.

Nutrients per Serving: *Calories: 160, Calories from Fat: 30%, Total Fat: 6 g, Saturated Fat: 1 g, Protein: 18 g, Carbohydrate: 10 g, Cholesterol: 22 mg, Sodium: 84 mg, Dietary Fiber: 3 g*

Dietary Exchanges: *2 Vegetable, 2 Lean Meat*

16

Meatballs in Creamy Mustard Sauce

1. Preheat oven to 400°F. Spray broiler pan with nonstick cooking spray.

2. Combine beef, bread crumbs, green onion, 1 tablespoon mustard, lemon pepper and salt in small bowl. Shape into 8 meatballs. Place in single layer on prepared broiler pan. Bake, uncovered, 15 minutes or until no longer pink in center.

3. Meanwhile, cook fettucine in medium saucepan according to package directions. Drain and keep warm.

4. Whisk together beef broth, remaining 1 teaspoon mustard and cornstarch in same saucepan until smooth. Cook over low heat, stirring constantly, until mixture comes to a boil. Remove from heat. Stir about 1 tablespoon broth mixture into sour cream. Stir sour cream mixture into broth mixture in saucepan. Heat over low heat 1 minute. *Do not boil.* Remove from heat; stir in meatballs.

5. Divide fettuccine between two serving plates and top with meatballs and sauce. Sprinkle with parsley, if desired. Serve immediately.   *Makes 2 servings*

Nutrients per Serving: *Calories: 318, Calories from Fat: 23%, Total Fat: 8 g, Saturated Fat: 3 g, Protein: 24 g, Carbohydrate: 37 g, Cholesterol: 52 mg, Sodium: 657 mg, Dietary Fiber: 2 g*

Dietary Exchanges: *2½ Starch, 2½ Lean Meat*

6 ounces 95% lean ground sirloin
⅓ cup fresh bread crumbs
2 tablespoons chopped green onion with tops
1 tablespoon plus 1 teaspoon Dijon mustard, divided
½ teaspoon lemon pepper
¼ teaspoon salt
3 ounces uncooked fettuccine or 1¼ cups tri-color rotini pasta
½ cup fat-free, reduced-sodium beef broth
2 teaspoons cornstarch
3 tablespoons reduced-fat sour cream
Minced fresh parsley (optional)

20 minutes or less

DINNER FOR ONE OR TWO

1 reduced-sodium
 bacon slice, cut
 crosswise into
 thirds
3 sea scallops
 (2 ounces)
2 ounces uncooked
 angel hair pasta
1 tablespoon
 reduced-fat
 margarine
2 green onions with
 tops, sliced
1 small clove garlic,
 minced
 Black pepper or
 garlic pepper, to
 taste

Bacon-Wrapped Scallops on Angel Hair Pasta

1. Wrap one bacon piece around each scallop; secure with toothpick.

2. Cook pasta according to package directions; drain. Return to pan.

3. Meanwhile, heat small nonstick skillet over medium heat. Add scallops; cook 2 to 3 minutes on each side or until bacon is crisp and browned and scallops are opaque. Remove scallops from skillet; discard toothpicks. Reduce heat to low.

4. Melt margarine in same skillet.* Add onion and garlic; cook and stir 1 minute or until onion is tender. Remove from heat.

5. Add onion mixture to pasta; toss lightly. Place on serving plate. Top with scallops. Season with pepper.

Makes 1 serving

*If there are enough drippings in the skillet after the bacon is cooked, you may not need the margarine for cooking the onion and garlic. Without the margarine calories are 245, total fat is 4 grams and percentage of calories from fat is 15.

Nutrients per Serving: *Calories: 305, Calories from Fat: 32%, Total Fat: 11 g, Saturated Fat: 2 g, Protein: 20 g, Carbohydrate: 32 g, Cholesterol: 93 mg, Sodium: 328 mg, Dietary Fiber: 2 g*

Dietary Exchanges: *2 Starch, 2 Lean Meat, 1 Fat*

1 tablespoon canola
    oil
¾ cup chopped
    peeled Granny
    Smith apple
⅓ cup thinly sliced
    carrot
¼ cup chopped
    onion
1 clove garlic,
    minced
1 tablespoon
    all-purpose flour
½ teaspoon curry
    powder
⅛ teaspoon salt
⅛ teaspoon black
    pepper
    Pinch ground
    cloves
¾ cup water
1 cup chopped
    cooked chicken
    breast
½ cup no-salt-added
    diced tomatoes,
    undrained
2 tablespoons
    minced fresh
    cilantro
4 refrigerated soft
    breadsticks
    (⅔ of 7-ounce
    package)
    Additional minced
    fresh cilantro
    (optional)

Curried Chicken Pot Pies

1. Preheat oven to 375°F. Spray two 1½-cup casseroles or ovenproof bowls with nonstick cooking spray.

2. Heat oil in medium skillet over medium-high heat. Add apple, carrot, onion and garlic. Cook and stir 3 to 4 minutes or until apple and onion are tender. Add flour, curry powder, salt, pepper and cloves. Cook and stir over medium heat 1 minute. Stir in water. Cook, stirring constantly, until liquid boils and thickens. Stir in chicken and tomatoes. Cook 3 to 4 minutes or until heated through. Stir in 2 tablespoons cilantro. Spoon into prepared casseroles.

3. Arrange 2 breadsticks over top of chicken mixture in each bowl. Sprinkle additional cilantro over tops, if desired.

4. Bake 15 to 17 minutes or until breadsticks are browned and filling is bubbly.   *Makes 2 servings*

Note: Leftover breadstick dough may be refrigerated in an airtight container and reserved for another use.

Nutrients per Serving: *Calories: 408, Calories from Fat: 27%, Total Fat: 12 g, Saturated Fat: 2 g, Protein: 23 g, Carbohydrate: 48 g, Cholesterol: 44 mg, Sodium: 685 mg, Dietary Fiber: 4 g*

Dietary Exchanges: *1 Vegetable, ½ Fruit, 2½ Starch, 2 Lean Meat, 1 Fat*

20 minutes or less

3 ounces lean
    ground turkey
1 tablespoon mild
    or medium salsa
1 tablespoon
    crushed baked
    tortilla chips
1 ounce reduced-fat
    Monterey Jack
    cheese slice
    (optional)
1 whole wheat
    hamburger bun,
    split
1 lettuce leaf
    Additional salsa

Grilled Salsa Turkey Burger

1. Combine turkey, 1 tablespoon salsa and chips in small bowl; mix lightly. Shape into patty. Lightly oil grid or broiler rack to prevent sticking.

2. Grill over medium-hot coals or broil 4 to 6 inches from heat 6 minutes on each side or until no longer pink in center, turning once. Top with cheese during last 2 minutes of cooking time, if desired. Place bun, cut sides down, on grill during last 2 minutes of grilling time to toast until lightly browned.

3. Cover bottom half of bun with lettuce; top with burger, additional salsa and top half of bun.

Makes 1 serving

Nutrients per Serving: *Calories: 302, Calories from Fat: 32%, Total Fat: 11 g, Saturated Fat: 3 g, Protein: 22 g, Carbohydrate: 10 g, Cholesterol: 63 mg, Sodium: 494 mg, Dietary Fiber: 2 g*

Dietary Exchanges: *2 Starch, 2 Lean Meat, 1 Fat*

Recipe Tip

When purchasing ground turkey, check the package label to be sure it contains only white meat. Ground turkey with dark meat and skin may be high in fat. Choose turkey that is at least 97% lean.

Baked Pasta Casserole

1. Preheat oven to 350°F. Cook pasta according to package directions; drain. Return pasta to saucepan.

2. Meanwhile, heat small nonstick skillet over medium-high heat. Add beef, onion, bell pepper and garlic; cook and stir 3 to 4 minutes or until beef is browned and vegetables are crisp-tender. Drain.

3. Add beef mixture, spaghetti sauce and black pepper to pasta in saucepan; mix well. Spoon mixture into 1-quart baking dish. Sprinkle with cheese.

4. Bake 15 minutes or until heated through. Serve with pepperoncini, if desired.   *Makes 2 servings*

Note: To make ahead, assemble casserole as directed through step 3. Cover and refrigerate several hours or overnight. When ready to serve, bake, uncovered, in preheated 350°F oven for 30 minutes or until heated through.

Nutrients per Serving: *Calories: 282, Calories from Fat: 23%, Total Fat: 7 g, Saturated Fat: 3 g, Protein: 16 g, Carbohydrate: 37 g, Cholesterol: 31 mg, Sodium: 368 mg, Dietary Fiber: 3 g*

Dietary Exchanges: *2 Vegetable, 2 Starch, 1 Lean Meat, 1 Fat*

1½ cups (3 ounces) uncooked wagon wheel or rotelle pasta
3 ounces 95% lean ground sirloin
2 tablespoons chopped onion
2 tablespoons chopped green bell pepper
1 clove garlic, minced
½ cup fat-free spaghetti sauce
Black pepper
2 tablespoons shredded Italian-style mozzarella and Parmesan cheese blend
Pepperoncini (optional)

Recipe Tip

Pepperoncini are slender 2- to 3-inch-long chilies that are usually pickled. They are slightly sweet and moderately hot. Look for them in the Italian section of your supermarket.

⅔ cup fresh or
   frozen corn
   kernels
¼ cup finely
   chopped onion
¼ cup finely
   chopped red
   bell pepper
2 cloves garlic,
   minced
1 teaspoon chopped
   fresh rosemary
   or ½ teaspoon
   crushed dried
   rosemary,
   divided
½ teaspoon salt,
   divided
¼ to ½ teaspoon
   black pepper,
   divided
2 tilapia fillets
   (4 ounces each)
1 teaspoon olive oil

Tilapia & Sweet Corn Baked in Parchment

1. Preheat oven to 400°F. Cut two 15-inch squares of parchment paper or heavy-duty foil; fold each piece in half diagonally.

2. Combine corn, onion, bell pepper, garlic, ½ teaspoon rosemary, ¼ teaspoon salt and half of black pepper in small bowl. Open parchment paper; spoon half of corn mixture on one side of each piece, spreading out slightly.

3. Arrange fillets on corn mixture. Brush fish with oil; sprinkle with remaining ½ teaspoon rosemary, ¼ teaspoon salt and black pepper.

4. To seal packets, fold other half of parchment over fish and corn. Fold and crimp along edges until completely sealed. Place packets on baking sheet.

5. Bake 15 minutes or until fish is opaque. Place packets on serving plates. Cut open packets; peel back paper.   *Makes 2 servings*

Nutrients per Serving: *Calories: 189, Calories from Fat: 21%, Total Fat: 5 g, Saturated Fat: <1 g, Protein: 24 g, Carbohydrate: 15 g, Cholesterol: 0 mg, Sodium: 622 mg, Dietary Fiber: 2 g*

Dietary Exchanges: *1 Starch, 3 Lean Meat*

Recipe Tip

For a special flavor, roast corn and red bell pepper on foil-lined baking sheet lightly sprayed with nonstick cooking spray in 450°F oven for 10 to 15 minutes or until slightly brown, stirring once. Then proceed with the recipe as directed above.

¾ cup cholesterol-
free egg
substitute
¼ cup plain nonfat
yogurt
¼ cup chopped
green onions
with tops
2 teaspoons all-
purpose flour
1 teaspoon dried
basil leaves
⅛ teaspoon salt
⅛ teaspoon black
pepper
¾ cup frozen
broccoli florets,
thawed and
drained
⅓ cup (3 ounces)
drained and
flaked water-
packed boneless
skinless canned
salmon
2 tablespoons
grated fresh
Parmesan
cheese
1 plum tomato,
thinly sliced
¼ cup fresh bread
crumbs

Crustless Salmon & Broccoli Quiche

1. Preheat oven to 375°F. Spray 6-cup rectangular casserole or 9-inch pie plate with nonstick cooking spray.

2. Combine egg substitute, yogurt, green onions, flour, basil, salt and pepper in medium bowl until well blended. Stir in broccoli, salmon and Parmesan cheese. Spread evenly in prepared casserole. Top with tomato slices. Sprinkle bread crumbs over top.

3. Bake 20 to 25 minutes or until knife inserted into center comes out clean. Let stand 5 minutes before serving. *Makes 2 servings*

Nutrients per Serving: *Calories: 227, Calories from Fat: 22%, Total Fat: 6 g, Saturated Fat: 2 g, Protein: 25 g, Carbohydrate: 20 g, Cholesterol: 25 mg, Sodium: 717 mg, Dietary Fiber: 5 g*

Dietary Exchanges: *1 Vegetable, 1 Starch, 2 Lean Meat, ½ Fat*

Recipe Tip

To make fresh bread crumbs, remove the crust from bread slices and tear bread into small pieces. Use any kind of bread, but day-old French and Italian bread make the best bread crumbs.

Grilled Chicken with Spicy Black Beans & Rice

1. Rub chicken with jerk seasonings. Grill over medium-hot coals 8 to 10 minutes or until no longer pink in center.

2. Meanwhile, heat oil in medium saucepan or skillet over medium heat. Add bell pepper and chipotle pepper; cook 7 to 8 minutes, stirring frequently, until peppers are soft.

3. Add rice, beans, pimiento and olives to saucepan. Cook until hot, about 3 minutes.

4. Serve bean mixture with chicken. Top bean mixture with onion and cilantro, if desired. Garnish with lime wedges.   *Makes 2 servings*

Nutrients per Serving: *Calories: 214, Calories from Fat: 18%, Total Fat: 5 g, Saturated Fat: 1 g, Protein: 17 g, Carbohydrate: 30 g, Cholesterol: 34 mg, Sodium: 436 mg, Dietary Fiber: 5 g*

Dietary Exchanges: *2 Starch, 1½ Lean Meat*

Recipe Tip

Chipotle peppers are actually dried smoked jalapeño peppers. They have a wrinkled, dark brown skin and a smoky sweet flavor.

---

1 boneless skinless chicken breast (about 4 ounces)
½ teaspoon jerk seasonings
½ teaspoon olive oil
¼ cup finely diced green bell pepper
2 teaspoons minced dried chipotle peppers
¾ cup hot cooked rice
½ cup canned rinsed and drained black beans
2 tablespoons diced pimiento
1 tablespoon chopped pimiento-stuffed green olives
1 tablespoon chopped onion
1 tablespoon chopped fresh cilantro (optional)
Lime wedges

5 Ingredients or Less

20 minutes or less

You'll be surprised how much flavor five ingredients can bring to a recipe.

Ravioli with Tomato Pesto

4 ounces frozen cheese ravioli
1¼ cups coarsely chopped plum tomatoes
¼ cup fresh basil leaves
2 teaspoons pine nuts
2 teaspoons olive oil
¼ teaspoon salt
⅛ teaspoon black pepper
1 tablespoon grated Parmesan cheese

1. Cook ravioli according to package directions; drain.

2. Meanwhile, combine tomatoes, basil, pine nuts, oil, salt and pepper in food processor. Process using on/off pulsing action just until ingredients are chopped. Serve over ravioli. Top with cheese.

Makes 2 servings

Nutrients per Serving: *Calories: 175, Calories from Fat: 34%, Total Fat: 10 g, Saturated Fat: 2 g, Protein: 10 g, Carbohydrate: 20 g, Cholesterol: 59 mg, Sodium: 459 mg, Dietary Fiber: 3 g*

Dietary Exchanges: *1 Vegetable, 1 Starch, 1 Lean Meat, ½ Fat*

Grilled Tropical Shrimp

¼ cup barbecue
    sauce
2 tablespoons
    pineapple juice
    or orange juice
10 ounces medium
    shrimp in shells
2 medium firm
    nectarines
6 green onions, cut
    into 2-inch
    lengths, or
    yellow onion
    wedges

1. Prepare grill for direct grilling. Stir together barbecue sauce and pineapple juice. Set aside.

2. Peel and devein shrimp. Cut each nectarine into 6 wedges. Thread shrimp, nectarines and green onions onto 4 long metal skewers.

3. Spray grill grid with nonstick cooking spray. Grill skewers over medium coals 4 to 5 minutes or until shrimp are opaque, turning once and brushing frequently with barbecue sauce.

Makes 2 servings

Nutrients per Serving: *Calories: 232, Calories from Fat: 7%, Total Fat: 2 g, Saturated Fat: <1 g, Protein: 25 g, Carbohydrate: 30 g, Cholesterol: 217 mg, Sodium: 712 mg, Dietary Fiber: 3 g*

Dietary Exchanges: *1½ Fruit, 2½ Lean Meat*

Recipe Tip

Although shrimp are high in cholesterol, they are naturally low in total fat and saturated fat, making them a good choice for a low-fat diet.

Spicy Caribbean Pork Medallions

6 ounces pork tenderloin
1 teaspoon Caribbean jerk seasoning
Nonstick olive oil cooking spray
⅓ cup pineapple juice
1 teaspoon brown mustard
½ teaspoon cornstarch

1. Cut tenderloin into ½-inch-thick slices. Place each slice between 2 pieces of plastic wrap. Pound to ¼-inch thickness. Rub both sides of pork pieces with jerk seasoning.

2. Lightly spray large nonstick skillet with cooking spray. Add pork. Cook over medium heat 2 to 3 minutes or until no longer pink, turning once. Remove from skillet. Keep warm.

3. Stir together pineapple juice, mustard and cornstarch until smooth. Add to skillet. Cook and stir over medium heat until mixture comes to a boil and thickens slightly. Spoon over pork.

Makes 2 servings

Nutrients per Serving: *Calories: 134, Calories from Fat: 23%, Total Fat: 3 g, Saturated Fat: 1 g, Protein: 18 g, Carbohydrate: 7 g, Cholesterol: 49 mg, Sodium: 319 mg, Dietary Fiber: <1 g*

Dietary Exchanges: *½ Fruit, 2 Lean Meat*

20 minutes or less

7 ounces pork
    tenderloin
    Nonstick olive oil
    cooking spray
4 green onions, cut
    into ½-inch
    pieces
2 tablespoons
    hoisin sauce or
    Asian plum
    sauce
1½ cups packaged
    cole slaw mix
4 (8-inch) fat-free
    flour tortillas,
    warmed

Easy Moo Shu Pork

1. Thinly slice pork. Lightly spray large nonstick skillet with cooking spray. Heat over medium-high heat. Add pork and green onions; stir-fry 2 to 3 minutes or until pork is no longer pink. Stir in hoisin sauce. Stir in cole slaw mix.

2. Spoon pork mixture onto tortillas. Wrap to enclose. Serve immediately.   *Makes 2 servings*

Note: To warm tortillas, stack and wrap loosely in plastic wrap. Microwave on HIGH for 15 to 20 seconds or until hot and pliable.

Nutrients per Serving: *Calories: 293, Calories from Fat: 13%, Total Fat: 4 g, Saturated Fat: 1 g, Protein: 26 g, Carbohydrate: 37 g, Cholesterol: 58 mg, Sodium: 672 mg, Dietary Fiber: 14 g*

Dietary Exchanges: *1 Vegetable, 2 Starch, 2 Lean Meat*

Recipe Tip
When you substitute fat-free flour tortillas for regular ones, you save 3 grams of fat per serving.

Grilled Portobello Mushroom Sandwich

1. Brush mushroom, bell pepper, onion, if desired, and cut sides of bun with some dressing; place vegetables over medium-hot coals. Grill 2 minutes.

2. Turn vegetables over; brush with dressing. Grill 2 minutes or until vegetables are tender. Remove bell pepper and onion from grill.

3. Place bun halves on grill. Turn mushroom top side up; brush with any remaining dressing and cover with cheese, if desired. Grill 1 minute or until cheese is melted and bun is lightly toasted.

4. Cut pepper into strips. Place mushroom on bottom half of bun; top with pepper strips and onion slice. Cover with top half of bun.   *Makes 1 serving*

Note: To broil, brush mushroom, bell pepper, onion, if desired, and cut sides of bun with dressing. Place vegetables on greased rack of broiler pan; set bun aside. Broil vegetables 4 to 6 inches from heat 3 minutes; turn over. Brush with dressing. Broil 3 minutes or until vegetables are tender. Place mushroom, top side up, on broiler pan; top with cheese. Place bun, cut sides up, on broiler pan. Broil 1 minute or until cheese is melted and bun is toasted. Assemble sandwich as directed above.

Nutrients per Serving: *Calories: 225, Calories from Fat: 22%, Total Fat: 6 g, Saturated Fat: 3 g, Protein: 15 g, Carbohydrate: 30 g, Cholesterol: 27 mg, Sodium: 729 mg, Dietary Fiber: 6 g*

Dietary Exchanges: *2 Starch, 1 Lean Meat, ½ Fat*

1 large portobello mushroom cap, cleaned and stem removed
¼ medium green bell pepper, halved
1 thin slice red onion (optional)
1 whole wheat hamburger bun, split
2 tablespoons fat-free Italian dressing
1 (1-ounce) reduced-fat part-skim mozzarella cheese slice, cut in half

Spiced Turkey with Fruit Salsa

6 ounces turkey
   breast
   tenderloin
2 teaspoons lime
   juice
1 teaspoon
   mesquite
   chicken
   seasoning blend
   or ground
   cumin
¼ cup chunky salsa
½ cup frozen pitted
   sweet cherries,
   thawed and cut
   into halves*

*Drained canned sweet
cherries may be substituted for
frozen cherries.

1. Prepare grill for direct grilling. Brush both sides of turkey with lime juice. Sprinkle with mesquite seasoning.

2. Grill turkey over medium coals 15 to 20 minutes or until turkey is no longer pink and juices run clear, turning once.

3. Meanwhile, stir together salsa and cherries.

4. Thinly slice turkey. Spoon salsa mixture over turkey.   *Makes 2 servings*

Nutrients per Serving: *Calories: 125, Calories from Fat: 13%, Total Fat: 2 g, Saturated Fat: 1 g, Protein: 16 g, Carbohydrate: 11 g, Cholesterol: 34 mg, Sodium: 264 mg, Dietary Fiber: 2 g*

Dietary Exchanges: *½ Fruit, 2 Lean Meat*

**Nonstick olive oil
  cooking spray
2 large poblano chili
  peppers
½ can (15½ ounces)
  black beans,
  drained and
  rinsed
½ cup cooked brown
  rice
⅓ cup chunky salsa
  (mild or
  medium)
⅓ cup shredded
  pepper Jack
  cheese or
  reduced-fat
  Cheddar cheese,
  divided**

Black Beans &
Rice-Stuffed Chilies

1. Preheat oven to 375°F. Lightly spray shallow baking pan with cooking spray. Cut thin slice from one side of each pepper; chop pepper slices. In medium saucepan cook peppers in boiling water 6 minutes. Drain and rinse with cold water. Remove and discard seeds and membranes.

2. Stir together beans, rice, salsa, chopped pepper and ¼ cup cheese. Spoon into peppers, mounding mixture. Place peppers in prepared pan. Cover with foil. Bake 12 to 15 minutes or until heated through.

3. Sprinkle with remaining cheese. Bake 2 minutes more or until cheese melts.   *Makes 2 servings*

Nutrients per Serving: *Calories: 289, Calories from Fat: 25%, Total Fat: 8 g, Saturated Fat: 4 g, Protein: 12 g, Carbohydrate: 38 g, Cholesterol: 20 mg, Sodium: 984 mg, Dietary Fiber: 10 g*

Dietary Exchanges: *1 Vegetable, 2 Starch, 1½ Fat*

Recipe Tip

Poblano chilies are dark green medium-sized chilies that range in flavor from mild to quite hot. Anaheim chilies may be substituted if you prefer a mild, sweet flavor.

3 ounces boneless skinless chicken breast

3 tablespoons reduced-fat Italian salad dressing, divided

½ cup fat-free reduced-sodium chicken broth

¼ cup uncooked rice

½ cup frozen broccoli and carrot blend, thawed

Grilled Chicken, Rice & Veggies

1. Place chicken and 1 tablespoon salad dressing in resealable plastic food storage bag. Seal bag; turn to coat. Marinate in refrigerator 1 hour.

2. Remove chicken from marinade; discard marinade. Grill chicken over medium-hot coals 8 to 10 minutes or until chicken is no longer pink in center.

3. Meanwhile, bring broth to a boil in small saucepan; add rice. Cover; reduce heat and simmer 15 minutes, stirring in vegetables during last 5 minutes of cooking. Remove from heat and stir in remaining 2 tablespoons dressing. Serve with chicken. *Makes 1 serving*

Nutrients per Serving: *Calories: 268, Calories from Fat: 23%, Total Fat: 7 g, Saturated Fat: 1 g, Protein: 26 g, Carbohydrate: 25 g, Cholesterol: 54 mg, Sodium: 516 mg, Dietary Fiber: 4 g*

Dietary Exchanges: *1 Vegetable, 1½ Starch, 2 Lean Meat*

Recipe Tip

A marinade that has been in contact with raw chicken should only be used as a dipping sauce if it has been brought to a boil and allowed to boil for 5 minutes. This will destroy any salmonella bacteria introduced by the chicken.

6 ounces beef flank steak

½ teaspoon Mexican seasoning blend or chili powder

⅛ teaspoon salt
Nonstick olive oil cooking spray

4 cups packaged mixed salad greens

1 can (11 ounces) mandarin orange sections, drained

2 tablespoons green taco sauce

Tex-Mex Flank Steak Salad

1. Very thinly slice steak across the grain. Combine beef slices, Mexican seasoning and salt.

2. Lightly spray large nonstick skillet with cooking spray. Heat over medium-high heat. Add steak strips. Cook and stir 1 to 2 minutes or to desired doneness.

3. Toss together greens and orange sections. Arrange on serving plates. Top with warm steak. Drizzle with taco sauce.   *Makes 2 servings*

Nutrients per Serving: *Calories: 240, Calories from Fat: 25%, Total Fat: 7 g, Saturated Fat: 3 g, Protein: 25 g, Carbohydrate: 21 g, Cholesterol: 37 mg, Sodium: 388 mg, Dietary Fiber: 2 g*

Dietary Exchanges: *2 Vegetable, 1 Fruit, 2 Lean Meat*

Recipe Tip

Flank steak is a lean cut of meat, making it an excellent choice for low-fat cooking. Cutting it across the grain into very thin strips helps to tenderize it.

Chicken & Wild Rice Skillet Dinner

1. Melt margarine in small skillet over medium-high heat. Add chicken; cook and stir 3 to 5 minutes or until no longer pink.

2. Meanwhile, measure ¼ cup of the rice and 1 tablespoon plus ½ teaspoon of the seasoning mix. Reserve remaining rice and seasoning mix for another use.

3. Add rice, seasoning, water and apricots to skillet; mix well. Bring to a boil. Cover and reduce heat to low; simmer 25 minutes or until liquid is absorbed and rice is tender. *Makes 1 serving*

Nutrients per Serving: *Calories: 314, Calories from Fat: 13%, Total Fat: 5 g, Saturated Fat: 1 g, Protein: 24 g, Carbohydrate: 44 g, Cholesterol: 52 mg, Sodium: 669 mg, Dietary Fiber: 3 g*

Dietary Exchanges: *3 Starch, 2 Lean Meat*

FIVE INGREDIENTS OR LESS

1 teaspoon reduced-fat margarine
2 ounces boneless skinless chicken breast, cut into strips
1 package (5 ounces) long-grain and wild rice mix with seasoning
½ cup water
3 dried apricots, cut up

Recipe Tip
Dried apricots are a good source of beta-carotene.

½ (16-ounce)
    package
    prepared
    polenta
Nonstick cooking
    spray
1⅓ cups chopped
    plum tomatoes
⅔ cup canned black
    beans or red
    kidney beans,
    rinsed and
    drained
2 tablespoons
    chopped fresh
    basil leaves
¼ teaspoon black
    pepper
2 tablespoons
    grated
    Parmesan
    cheese

Polenta with Fresh Tomato-Bean Salsa

1. Preheat oven to 450°F. Cut polenta into ¼-inch-thick slices. Lightly spray shallow baking pan with cooking spray. Place polenta slices in single layer in baking pan. Lightly spray top of polenta with cooking spray. Bake 15 to 20 minutes or until slightly brown on edges.

2. Meanwhile, stir together tomatoes, beans, basil and pepper. Let stand at room temperature 15 minutes to blend flavors.

3. Arrange polenta on serving plates. Spoon tomato mixture on top. Sprinkle with cheese.

Makes 2 servings

Nutrients per Serving: *Calories: 286, Calories from Fat: 17%, Total Fat: 6 g, Saturated Fat: 2 g, Protein: 14 g, Carbohydrate: 48 g, Cholesterol: 9 mg, Sodium: 548 mg, Dietary Fiber: 8 g*

Dietary Exchanges: *1 Vegetable, 3 Starch, 1 Fat*

Recipe Tip

Salsa may be cooked, if desired. Cook and stir tomatoes in large skillet over medium heat until hot. Stir in basil and pepper. Serve as directed.

20 minutes or less

Nonstick olive oil
  cooking spray
6 ounces boneless
  skinless chicken
  breasts, cut into
  bite-size pieces
⅓ cup mango
  chutney
¼ cup water
1 tablespoon Dijon
  mustard
4 cups packaged
  mixed salad
  greens
1 cup chopped
  peeled mango
  or papaya
Sliced green
  onions
  (optional)

Warm Chutney Chicken Salad

1. Spray medium nonstick skillet with cooking spray. Heat over medium-high heat. Add chicken; cook and stir 2 to 3 minutes or until no longer pink. Stir in chutney, water and mustard. Cook and stir just until hot. Cool slightly.

2. Toss together salad greens and mango. Arrange on serving plates.

3. Spoon chicken mixture onto greens. Garnish with green onions, if desired. *Makes 2 servings*

Nutrients per Serving: *Calories: 277, Calories from Fat: 10%, Total Fat: 3 g, Saturated Fat: 1 g, Protein: 21 g, Carbohydrate: 42 g, Cholesterol: 52 mg, Sodium: 117 mg, Dietary Fiber: 4 g*

Dietary Exchanges: *2 Vegetable, 2 Fruit, 2 Lean Meat*

Recipe Tip

Mango chutney is a spicy, chunky condiment most often used as an accompaniment to Indian curries. It ranges in spiciness from mild to hot.

Two-for-One Dinners

20 minutes or less

Save part of today's recipe and create something new tomorrow.

Jerk Turkey Salad

Reserved turkey from Jamaican Jerk Turkey
 Wraps (page 50)
4 cups packaged mixed salad greens
¾ cup sliced peeled cucumber
⅔ cup chopped fresh pineapple
⅔ cup quartered strawberries or raspberries
½ cup slivered peeled jicama or sliced celery
1 green onion, sliced
¼ cup lime juice
3 tablespoons honey

1. Cut reserved turkey into bite-size pieces. Toss together greens, turkey, cucumber, pineapple, strawberries, jicama and green onion.

2. Combine lime juice and honey. Toss with greens mixture. Serve immediately.   *Makes 2 servings*

Nutrients per Serving: *Calories: 265, Calories from Fat: 6%, Total Fat: 2 g, Saturated Fat: 1 g, Protein: 17 g, Carbohydrate: 48 g, Cholesterol: 34 mg, Sodium: 356 mg, Dietary Fiber: 6 g*

Dietary Exchanges: *2 Vegetable, 2 Fruit, 2 Lean Meat*

¾ pound turkey
   breast
   tenderloin
1 tablespoon
   Caribbean jerk
   seasoning
2 cups broccoli slaw
1 small tomato,
   seeded and
   chopped (about
   ⅔ cup)
3 tablespoons
   reduced-fat
   coleslaw
   dressing
1 jalapeño pepper,*
   finely chopped
1 tablespoon
   mustard
   (optional)
4 (8-inch) fat-free
   flour tortillas,
   warmed

*Jalapeño peppers can sting
and irritate the skin; wear
rubber gloves when handling
peppers and do not touch
eyes. Wash hands after
handling.

Jamaican Jerk Turkey Wraps

1. Prepare grill for direct grilling. Rub jerk seasoning on both sides of turkey.

2. Grill turkey over medium coals 15 to 20 minutes or until turkey is no longer pink and juices run clear, turning once. Thinly slice half of turkey. Cover and refrigerate remaining turkey; reserve for Jerk Turkey Salad (page 48).

3. Toss together broccoli slaw, tomato, dressing, jalapeño pepper and mustard. Place sliced turkey on tortillas; spoon broccoli slaw mixture on top. Wrap to enclose. Serve immediately.   *Makes 2 servings*

Nutrients per Serving: *Calories: 356, Calories from Fat: 30%, Total Fat: 12 g, Saturated Fat: 2 g, Protein: 20 g, Carbohydrate: 40 g, Cholesterol: 41 mg, Sodium: 1058 mg, Dietary Fiber: 15 g*

Dietary Exchanges: *2 Vegetable, 2 Starch, 2 Lean Meat, 1 Fat*

Recipe Tip

Broccoli slaw, which is slivered broccoli stalks, is now available in most supermarkets. Add it to wraps or pita bread sandwiches, or toss it with coleslaw dressing for a nutritious salad.

50

Thai Curry Stir-Fry

¾ cup fat-free, reduced-sodium chicken broth

1 tablespoon cornstarch

2 teaspoons curry powder

1 tablespoon reduced-sodium soy sauce

¼ teaspoon crushed red pepper

Nonstick olive oil cooking spray

4 green onions, sliced

1 to 2 cloves garlic, minced

3 cups broccoli florets

1 cup sliced carrot

2 teaspoons olive oil

10 ounces boneless skinless chicken breasts, cut into bite-size pieces

⅔ cup hot cooked rice, prepared without salt

1. Stir together broth, cornstarch, curry powder, soy sauce and red pepper. Set aside.

2. Spray nonstick wok or large nonstick skillet with cooking spray. Heat over medium-high heat. Add green onions and garlic; stir-fry 1 minute. Remove from wok.

3. Add broccoli and carrot to wok; stir-fry 2 to 3 minutes or until crisp-tender. Remove from wok.

4. Add oil to hot wok. Add chicken and stir-fry 2 to 3 minutes or until no longer pink. Stir broth mixture. Add to wok. Cook and stir until broth mixture comes to a boil and thickens slightly. Return all vegetables to wok. Heat through.

5. Cover and refrigerate 1½ cups of chicken mixture. Reserve for Curried Chicken & Pasta Salad (page 54).

6. Serve remaining chicken mixture with rice.

Makes 2 servings

Nutrients per Serving: Calories: 273, Calories from Fat: 20%, Total Fat: 6 g, Saturated Fat: 1 g, Protein: 28 g, Carbohydrate: 27 g, Cholesterol: 57 mg, Sodium: 308 mg, Dietary Fiber: 5 g

Dietary Exchanges: 2 Vegetable, 1 Starch, 3 Lean Meat

1½ cups reserved
  chicken mixture
  from Thai Curry
  Stir-Fry (page 52)
⅔ cup cooked small
  shell pasta
½ cup sliced celery
⅓ cup dried
  cranberries or
  tart cherries
¼ cup fat-free honey
  Dijon salad
  dressing
  Salt
2 lettuce leaves

Curried Chicken & Pasta Salad

1. Toss together reserved chicken mixture, pasta, celery, cranberries and salad dressing. Season to taste with salt.

2. Cover and refrigerate 1 to 24 hours. Serve on lettuce leaves.   *Makes 2 servings*

Nutrients per Serving: *Calories: 322, Calories from Fat: 11%, Total Fat: 4 g, Saturated Fat: 1 g, Protein: 18 g, Carbohydrate: 55 g, Cholesterol: 29 mg, Sodium: 517 mg, Dietary Fiber: 5 g*

Dietary Exchanges: *2 Vegetable, 3 Starch, 1 Lean Meat*

Recipe Tip

Skinless, well-trimmed chicken or turkey breast is lower in fat than all meat products, making it an excellent choice for a low-fat diet.

Pork, Mushrooms, Onion & Pepper

1. Sprinkle both sides of pork chops with salt and garlic pepper. Coat large nonstick skillet with cooking spray; heat over medium-low heat. Cook pork 1 to 2 minutes per side side or until brown and barely pink in center. Remove from skillet. Cover and refrigerate half the pork; reserve for Pork & Vegetable Wraps (page 56). Keep remaining pork warm.

2. Heat oil over medium heat in same nonstick skillet. Add mushrooms, onion, bell pepper, garlic and salt. Cook 8 to 10 minutes or until vegetables are soft. Add wine, a little at a time, stirring to remove any browned bits from bottom of skillet. Bring to a boil; boil 2 minutes. Serve vegetable mixture over pork chops. *Makes 2 servings*

1 pound boneless thin-cut pork loin chops
⅛ teaspoon salt
¼ teaspoon garlic pepper
Nonstick cooking spray
1 teaspoon olive oil
1½ cups thinly sliced mushrooms
1 cup diced onion
1 cup diced red bell pepper
1 clove garlic, minced
⅛ teaspoon salt
¼ cup red wine

Nutrients per Serving: *Calories: 264, Calories from Fat: 34%, Total Fat: 10 g, Saturated Fat: 3 g, Protein: 22 g, Carbohydrate: 18 g, Cholesterol: 40 mg, Sodium: 340 mg, Dietary Fiber: 4 g*

Dietary Exchanges: *3 Vegetable, 3 Starch, ½ Fat*

Recipe Tip

Wine adds a lot of flavor to recipes. Just be sure that wine mixtures cook for 2 or 3 minutes to burn off the alcohol and allow flavors to blend.

8 ounces reserved
    cooked boneless
    thin-cut pork
    chops from
    Pork,
    Mushrooms,
    Onion & Pepper
    (page 55)
1 tablespoon
    reduced-fat
    mayonnaise
2 teaspoons Dijon
    mustard
4 (8-inch) fat-free
    flour tortillas
1 cup torn spinach
    leaves
½ peeled cucumber,
    diced
1 medium tomato,
    chopped
    Black pepper to
    taste
    Celery salt
    (optional)

Pork & Vegetable Wraps

1. Cut pork chops into strips. Combine mayonnaise and mustard in small cup. Spread on one side of each tortilla. Top with remaining ingredients, seasoning to taste with pepper and celery salt, if desired.

2. Fold in 2 sides of tortilla and roll up to enclose filling. Lay seam side down and cut in half. Serve immediately.   *Makes 2 servings*

Nutrients per Serving: *Calories: 327, Calories from Fat: 30%, Total Fat: 11 g, Saturated Fat: 3 g, Protein: 24 g, Carbohydrate: 33 g, Cholesterol: 40 mg, Sodium: 637 mg, Dietary Fiber: 14 g*

Dietary Exchanges: *3 Vegetable, 1 Starch, 3 Lean Meat, ½ Fat*

Recipe Tip

The mayonnaise-mustard mixture in this recipe may be served on the side as a dipping sauce rather than spread on the tortillas, if desired.

20 minutes or less

12 ounces ground
    sirloin
½ cup chopped
    onion
2 cloves garlic,
    minced
1 can (8 ounces)
    tomato sauce
⅓ cup chopped
    carrot
¼ cup water
2 tablespoons red
    wine
1 teaspoon dried
    Italian
    seasoning
1½ cups hot cooked
    penne pasta
Chopped fresh
    parsley

Bolognese Sauce & Penne Pasta

1. Heat medium saucepan over medium heat until hot. Add beef, onion and garlic; cook and stir 5 to 7 minutes, breaking up meat with spoon, until beef is browned. Remove ½ cup of beef mixture and refrigerate; reserve for Speedy Tacos (page 59).

2. To beef mixture remaining in saucepan, add tomato sauce, carrot, water, wine and Italian seasoning. Bring to a boil. Reduce heat and simmer 15 minutes. Place pasta in bowls and top with sauce. Sprinkle with parsley.   *Makes 2 servings*

Nutrients per Serving: *Calories: 292, Calories from Fat: 14%, Total Fat: 5 g, Saturated Fat: 2 g, Protein: 21 g, Carbohydrate: 40 g, Cholesterol: 45 mg, Sodium: 734 mg, Dietary Fiber: 4 g*

Dietary Exchanges: *1 Vegetable, 2 Starch, 2 Lean Meat*

Recipe Tip

Carrots add sweetness that reduces the acidic flavor of this quick bolognese sauce.

Speedy Tacos

20 minutes or less

1. In small saucepan, heat beef, tomato sauce and seasonings until hot.

2. Warm taco shells in oven following package directions.

3. Fill taco shells with meat mixture, cheese, lettuce, tomato and onion. Serve with pepper sauce, if desired.   *Makes 2 servings*

Nutrients per Serving *(3 tacos): Calories: 342, Calories from Fat: 36%, Total Fat: 14 g, Saturated Fat: 4 g, Protein: 19 g, Carbohydrate: 36 g, Cholesterol: 40 mg, Sodium: 706 mg, Dietary Fiber: 5 g*

Dietary Exchanges: *1 Vegetable, 2 Starch, 2 Lean Meat, 1½ Fat*

Recipe Tip

If you wish to reduce the fat in these easy tacos, simply divide the filling among 4 taco shells instead of 6.

½ cup reserved cooked beef mixture from Bolognese Sauce & Penne Pasta (page 58)

⅓ cup no-salt-added tomato sauce

1 tablespoon taco seasonings

6 taco shells

¼ cup (2 ounces) shredded reduced-fat Cheddar cheese

½ cup shredded lettuce

⅓ cup diced tomato

¼ cup chopped onion

Hot pepper sauce (optional)

4 ears fresh corn,
  unhusked
1 (12-ounce) salmon
  fillet, cut into
  4 pieces
2 tablespoons plus
  1 teaspoon
  fresh lime juice,
  divided
1 clove garlic,
  minced
1 teaspoon chili
  powder
½ teaspoon ground
  cumin
½ teaspoon oregano
  leaves
¼ teaspoon salt,
  divided
⅛ teaspoon black
  pepper
2 teaspoons
  margarine,
  melted
2 teaspoons minced
  fresh cilantro

Southwest Roasted Salmon & Corn

1. Preheat oven to 400°F. Spray shallow 1-quart baking dish with nonstick cooking spray. Pull back husks from each ear of corn, leaving husks attached. Discard silk. Soak ears in cold water 20 minutes.

2. Place salmon, skin sides down, in prepared baking dish. Pour 2 tablespoons lime juice over fillets. Marinate at room temperature 15 minutes.

3. Combine garlic, chili powder, cumin, oregano, ⅛ teaspoon salt and pepper in small bowl. Pat salmon lightly with paper towel to dry. Rub garlic mixture on tops and sides of salmon.

4. Remove corn from water; pat kernels dry with paper towels. Bring husks back up over each ear; secure at top with thin strips of corn husk. Place corn on 1 side of oven rack. Roast 10 minutes. Turn over with tongs.

5. Place salmon on other side of oven rack. Roast 15 minutes or until salmon is opaque and flakes when tested with fork, and corn is tender.

6. Combine margarine, cilantro and remaining ⅛ teaspoon salt in small bowl. Remove husks from corn. Brush over two ears of corn.

7. Set aside two ears of corn and two pieces of salmon. Wrap and refrigerate. Reserve for Salmon, Corn & Barley Chowder (page 62). Serve remaining seasoned corn and salmon.   *Makes 2 servings*

Nutrients per Serving: *Calories: 186, Calories from Fat: 29%, Total Fat: 6 g, Saturated Fat: 1 g, Protein: 19 g, Carbohydrate: 16 g, Cholesterol: 43 mg, Sodium: 243 mg, Dietary Fiber: 2 g*

Dietary Exchanges: *1 Starch, 1 Lean Meat*

Salmon, Corn & Barley Chowder

1 teaspoon canola oil
¼ cup chopped onion
1 clove garlic, minced
2½ cups fat-free reduced-sodium chicken broth
¼ cup quick-cooking barley
1 tablespoon water
1 tablespoon all-purpose flour
2 reserved ears of corn from Southwest Roasted Salmon & Corn (page 60)
6 ounces reserved salmon from Southwest Roasted Salmon & Corn (page 60)
⅓ cup reduced-fat (2%) milk
1 tablespoon minced cilantro
Black pepper
Lime wedges

1. Heat oil in medium saucepan over medium heat until hot. Add onion and garlic. Cook and stir 1 to 2 minutes or until onion is tender.

2. Add broth and bring to a boil. Stir in barley. Cover; reduce heat to low. Simmer 10 minutes or until barley is tender.

3. Stir water slowly into flour in cup until smooth.

4. Cut kernels from ears of corn. Break salmon into chunks.

5. Add corn, salmon and milk to saucepan, stirring to blend. Stir in flour mixture. Simmer gently 2 to 3 minutes or until slightly thickened. Stir in cilantro and pepper. Serve with lime wedges.

Makes 2 (2¼-cup) servings

Nutrients per Serving: *Calories: 321, Calories from Fat: 20%, Total Fat: 7 g, Saturated Fat: 1 g, Protein: 26 g, Carbohydrate: 40 g, Cholesterol: 46 mg, Sodium: 310 mg, Dietary Fiber: 7 g*

Dietary Exchanges: *3 Starch, 2 Lean Meat*

Recipe Tip

Cilantro is a fresh leafy herb that has a distinctive flavor and pungent aroma. Its flavor complements spicy foods, especially Mexican, Caribbean, Thai and Vietnamese dishes.

2 cups diced green
    bell peppers
2 cups thinly sliced
    carrots
2 cups thin onion
    wedges
1 pound
    mushrooms, cut
    into halves*
4 cloves garlic,
    chopped
2 tablespoons
    balsamic or red
    wine vinegar
2 teaspoons olive
    oil
¼ teaspoon salt,
    divided
¼ teaspoon black
    pepper, divided
1 tablespoon
    country-style
    Dijon mustard
1 turkey tenderloin
    (12 ounces)
1 teaspoon paprika
    Nonstick cooking
    spray

*Cut large mushrooms into
quarters.

Turkey Tenderloin with Caramelized Vegetables

1. Preheat oven to 400°F. Line 15×10-inch baking pan with heavy-duty foil.

2. Combine bell peppers, carrots, onions, mushrooms, garlic, vinegar, oil, ⅛ teaspoon salt and ⅛ teaspoon pepper in large bowl, tossing to coat vegetables evenly with seasonings. Spread vegetables onto prepared pan. Bake 15 minutes.

3. Meanwhile, spread mustard over top of turkey. Combine paprika, remaining ⅛ teaspoon salt and ⅛ teaspoon pepper in small bowl. Sprinkle over turkey. Lightly spray top of turkey with cooking spray.

4. Remove vegetables from oven. Stir vegetables and push to edges of pan. Place turkey in center of vegetables.

5. Roast 20 minutes. Stir vegetables. Roast 20 minutes more or until turkey is no longer pink in center (170°F). Let turkey stand 5 minutes. Carve half of turkey across the grain into ½-inch-thick slices. Reserve remaining turkey for Turkey Paprikash (page 65).

6. Divide sliced turkey between two plates. Place 1 cup vegetables on each plate. Reserve remaining vegetables for Turkey Paprikash (page 65).

Makes 2 servings

Nutrients per Serving: *Calories: 232, Calories from Fat: 18%, Total Fat: 5 g, Saturated Fat: 1 g, Protein: 20 g, Carbohydrate: 30 g, Cholesterol: 34 mg, Sodium: 215 mg, Dietary Fiber: 7 g*

Dietary Exchanges: *4 Vegetable, 2 Lean Meat*

Turkey Paprikash

1. Cook noodles according to package directions, omitting salt. Drain and keep warm.

2. Meanwhile, spray medium skillet with cooking spray. Heat over medium heat until hot. Add garlic and paprika. Cook and stir 30 seconds or until garlic is fragrant. Stir in water, tomato paste, salt and pepper. Simmer, uncovered, 5 minutes.

3. Stir in leftover turkey and vegetables. Cover; simmer 5 minutes or until heated through. Remove from heat; stir in sour cream and noodles. Top each serving with parsley.   *Makes 2 servings*

Nutrients per Serving: *Calories: 330, Calories from Fat: 19%, Total Fat: 7 g, Saturated Fat: 3 g, Protein: 26 g, Carbohydrate: 43 g, Cholesterol: 47 mg, Sodium: 484 mg, Dietary Fiber: 8 g*

Dietary Exchanges: *3 Vegetable, 2 Starch, 2 Lean Meat*

Recipe Tip

For added flavor in this recipe, add tomato paste to the skillet after cooking garlic. Cook the tomato paste for 2 or 3 minutes before adding water and seasonings, then proceed with recipe as directed.

---

1 cup yolk-free extra-broad noodles
Nonstick cooking spray
2 cloves garlic, minced
2 teaspoons paprika
¾ cup water
1½ tablespoons tomato paste
⅛ teaspoon salt
⅛ teaspoon black pepper
4 ounces reserved Turkey Tenderloin (page 64), cut into ½-inch pieces
1¾ cups reserved Caramelized Vegetables (page 64)
3 tablespoons reduced-fat sour cream
2 teaspoons minced fresh parsley

Meatless Dinners

20 minutes or less

Need a change of pace? Try one of these tasty meatless meals.

Grilled Mozzarella & Roasted Red Pepper Sandwich

1 tablespoon reduced-fat olive oil vinaigrette or Italian salad dressing
2 slices (2 ounces) Italian-style sandwich bread
⅓ cup bottled roasted red peppers, rinsed, drained and patted dry
   Basil leaves (optional)
2 ounces part-skim mozzarella or reduced-fat Swiss cheese slices
   Nonstick olive oil cooking spray

1. Brush dressing on one side of one slice of bread; top with peppers, basil, if desired, cheese and second bread slice. Lightly spray both sides of sandwich with cooking spray.

2. Heat skillet over medium heat. Place sandwich in skillet; grill 4 to 5 minutes per side until brown and cheese is melted.   *Makes 1 serving*

Nutrients per Serving: *Calories: 303, Calories from Fat: 29%, Total Fat: 9 g, Saturated Fat: 5 g, Protein: 16 g, Carbohydrate: 35 g, Cholesterol: 25 mg, Sodium: 727 mg, Dietary Fiber: 2 g*

Dietary Exchanges: *1 Vegetable, 2 Starch, 1 Lean Meat, 1½ Fat*

Grilled Mozzarella & Roasted Red Pepper Sandwich

1 teaspoon olive oil
¼ cup diced green
    bell pepper
¼ cup diced zucchini
¼ cup sliced
    mushrooms
¼ cup diced carrot
¼ cup sliced green
    onions
2 cloves garlic,
    minced
1 plum tomato,
    diced
1 tablespoon red
    wine or water
½ teaspoon dried
    basil leaves
¼ teaspoon salt
⅛ teaspoon black
    pepper
2 cups cooked
    spaghetti
    squash
2 tablespoons
    grated
    Parmesan
    cheese

Spaghetti Squash Primavera

1. Heat oil in medium skillet over low heat. Add bell pepper, zucchini, mushrooms, carrot, green onions and garlic; cook 10 to 12 minutes or until crisp-tender, stirring ocassionally. Stir in tomato, wine, basil, salt and black pepper; cook 4 to 5 minutes, stirring once or twice.

2. Serve vegetables over spaghetti squash. Top with cheese.   *Makes 2 servings*

Nutrients per Serving: *Calories: 116, Calories from Fat: 32%, Total Fat: 5 g, Saturated Fat: 1 g, Protein: 5 g, Carbohydrate: 15 g, Cholesterol: 4 mg, Sodium: 396 mg, Dietary Fiber: 5 g*

Dietary Exchanges: *3 Vegetable, 1 Fat*

Recipe Tip

To cook spaghetti squash, cut the squash in half lengthwise. Remove and discard seeds. Place squash, cut side down, in a 13×9-inch baking dish sprayed with nonstick cooking spray. Bake at 350°F for 45 minutes to 1 hour or until tender. Using a fork, remove spaghetti-like strands from hot squash.

Nonstick cooking
spray
1 teaspoon olive oil
¾ cup thinly sliced
fennel bulb
¾ cup thinly sliced
onion
2 cloves garlic,
minced
¾ cup cooked brown
rice
2 tablespoons
balsamic
vinegar, divided
2 teaspoons Italian
seasoning,
divided
3 ounces firm tofu,
crumbled
¼ cup crumbled feta
cheese
6 ounces ripe plum
tomatoes, sliced
¼ inch thick
6 ounces zucchini,
sliced ¼ inch
thick
⅛ teaspoon salt
⅛ teaspoon black
pepper
¼ cup fresh bread
crumbs
2 tablespoons
grated fresh
Parmesan
cheese

Vegetable & Tofu Gratin

1. Preheat oven to 400°F. Spray 1-quart shallow baking dish with nonstick cooking spray.

2. Spray medium skillet with cooking spray. Heat oil in skillet over medium heat until hot. Add fennel and onion. Cook about 10 minutes or until tender and lightly browned, stirring frequently. Add garlic; cook and stir 1 minute. Spread over bottom of prepared baking dish.

3. Combine rice, 1 tablespoon vinegar and ½ teaspoon Italian seasoning in small bowl. Spread over onion mixture.

4. Combine tofu, feta cheese, remaining 1 tablespoon vinegar and 1 teaspoon Italian seasoning in same small bowl; toss to combine. Spoon over rice.

5. Top with alternating rows of tomato and zucchini slices. Sprinkle with salt and pepper.

6. Combine bread crumbs, Parmesan cheese and remaining ½ teaspoon Italian seasoning in small bowl. Sprinkle over top. Spray bread crumb topping lightly with nonstick cooking spray. Bake 30 minutes or until heated through and topping is browned.

Makes 2 servings

Nutrients per Serving: *Calories: 399, Calories from Fat: 30%, Total Fat: 14 g, Saturated Fat: 5 g, Protein: 19 g, Carbohydrate: 52 g, Cholesterol: 19 mg, Sodium: 460 mg, Dietary Fiber: 7 g*

Dietary Exchanges: *2 Vegetable, 3 Starch, 3 Fat*

1 teaspoon olive oil
½ cup diced red bell
   pepper
¼ cup diced onion
1¼ teaspoons curry
   powder
1 clove garlic,
   minced
½ teaspoon salt
1¼ cups peeled,
   cubed eggplant
¾ cup peeled, cubed
   acorn or
   butternut
   squash
⅔ cup rinsed and
   drained canned
   chick-peas
½ cup vegetable
   broth or water
3 tablespoons white
   wine
   Hot pepper sauce
   (optional)
¼ cup lemon-
   flavored sugar-
   free yogurt
2 tablespoons
   chopped fresh
   parsley

Curried Eggplant, Squash & Chick-Pea Stew

1. Heat oil in medium saucepan over medium heat. Add bell pepper and onion; cook and stir 5 minutes. Stir in curry powder, garlic and salt. Add eggplant, squash, chick-peas, broth and wine to saucepan. Cover; bring to a boil. Reduce heat and simmer 20 to 25 minutes just until squash and eggplant are tender.

2. Season to taste with pepper sauce, if desired. Serve with yogurt and parsley.   *Makes 2 servings*

Nutrients per Serving: *Calories: 216, Calories from Fat: 14%, Total Fat: 4 g, Saturated Fat: <1 g, Protein: 7 g, Carbohydrate: 38g, Cholesterol: 0 mg, Sodium: 47 mg, Dietary Fiber: 10 g*

Dietary Exchanges: *2½ Starch, 1 Fat*

Recipe Tip

Foods that are high in fiber, such as beans, whole grains, fruit and vegetables, may help lower blood glucose levels slightly in some individuals with type 2 diabetes.

French Bread Portobello Pizza

1. Preheat oven to 450°F. Spray small skillet with cooking spray. Heat over medium-low heat until hot. Cook and stir mushroom and garlic 5 to 7 minutes or until mushroom is slightly soft.

2. Stir in tomato and tomato sauce; cook 5 minutes. Spread mixture over cut sides of bread. Sprinkle with cheese. Bake 15 minutes until cheese is melted. Sprinkle with pepper flakes, if desired.

Makes 1 serving

Nutrients per Serving: *Calories: 246, Calories from Fat: 13%, Total Fat: 4 g, Saturated Fat: 1 g, Protein: 15 g, Carbohydrate: 39 g, Cholesterol: 4 mg, Sodium: 661 mg, Dietary Fiber: 4 g*

Dietary Exchanges: *2 Vegetable, 2 Starch, 1 Lean Meat*

Nonstick cooking spray
⅓ cup sliced portobello mushroom
1 clove garlic, minced
½ cup chopped tomato
1 tablespoon tomato sauce
1 (2-ounce) piece French bread, cut in half lengthwise
¼ cup (1 ounce) shredded reduced-fat Italian blend or part-skim mozzarella cheese
Red pepper flakes (optional)

Recipe Tip

Portobello mushrooms have very large dark brown caps and thick, tough stems. Because they have a firm texture when cooked, they are sometimes substituted for beef in vegetarian dishes. Baby portobello mushrooms, which are available in some produce markets, are a good choice for this recipe.

20 minutes or less

2 tablespoons fresh
  lime juice
1½ teaspoons canola
  oil
½ teaspoon ground
  cumin
½ teaspoon water
⅛ teaspoon salt
¾ cup canned red
  beans, rinsed
  and drained
½ cup frozen corn
  with bell
  pepper and
  onion, thawed
¼ cup chopped
  tomato
2 tablespoons
  chopped green
  onion, divided
2 large romaine
  lettuce leaves

MEATLESS DINNERS

Red Bean & Corn Salad with Lime-Cumin Dressing

1. Whisk together lime juice, oil, cumin, water and salt in medium bowl.

2. Add beans, corn, tomato and 1 tablespoon green onion; toss to coat. Serve on lettuce leaves. Top with remaining green onion.   *Makes 1 serving*

Nutrients per Serving: *Calories: 198, Calories from Fat: 18%, Total Fat: 4 g, Saturated Fat: <1 g, Protein: 8 g, Carbohydrate: 33 g, Cholesterol: 0 mg, Sodium: 908 mg, Dietary Fiber: 9 g*

Dietary Exchanges: *2 Starch, 1 Lean Meat*

Red Bean & Corn Salad with Lime-Cumin Dressing

Cheesy Baked Barley

2 cups water
½ cup medium pearled barley
½ teaspoon salt, divided
Nonstick cooking spray
½ cup diced onion
½ cup diced zucchini
½ cup diced red bell pepper
1½ teaspoons all-purpose flour
Seasoned pepper
¾ cup fat-free (skim) milk
1 cup (4 ounces) shredded reduced-fat Italian blend cheese, divided
1 tablespoon Dijon mustard

1. Bring water to a boil in 1-quart saucepan. Add barley and ¼ teaspoon salt. Cover and reduce heat. Simmer 45 minutes or until tender and most water is evaporated. Let stand, covered, 5 minutes.

2. Preheat oven to 375°F. Spray medium skillet with cooking spray. Cook onion, zucchini and bell pepper over medium-low heat about 10 minutes or until soft. Stir in flour, remaining ¼ teaspoon salt and seasoned pepper; cook 1 to 2 minutes. Add milk, stirring constantly; cook and stir until slightly thickened. Remove from heat and add barley, ¾ cup cheese and mustard; stir until cheese is melted.

3. Spread in even layer in casserole. Sprinkle with remaining ¼ cup cheese. Bake 20 minutes or until hot. Preheat broiler. Broil casserole 1 to 2 minutes until cheese is lightly browned.   *Makes 2 servings*

Nutrients per Serving: *Calories: 362, Calories from Fat: 23%, Total Fat: 9 g, Saturated Fat: 4 g, Protein: 20 g, Carbohydrate: 50 g, Cholesterol: 32 mg, Sodium: 1159 mg, Dietary Fiber: 6 g*

Dietary Exchanges: *2 Vegetable, 2½ Starch, 2 Lean Meat, ½ Fat*

Recipe Tip

Barley is an excellent substitute for rice. When cooked, it has a slightly chewy texture and mild nutty flavor. Not only does it have four times the fiber of white rice, but barley also contains 20 percent less carbohydrate than white rice.

Cheesy Baked Barley

⅔ cup orange juice
3 tablespoons
    reduced-sodium
    soy sauce
½ to 1 teaspoon
    minced ginger
1 clove garlic,
    minced
¼ teaspoon red
    pepper flakes
5 ounces extra-firm
    tofu, well
    drained and cut
    into ½-inch
    cubes
1½ teaspoons
    cornstarch
1 teaspoon canola
    or peanut oil
2 cups fresh cut-up
    vegetables, such
    as broccoli,
    carrot, onion
    and snow peas
1½ cups hot cooked
    vermicelli pasta

Orange Ginger Tofu & Noodles

1. Combine orange juice, soy sauce, ginger, garlic and red pepper in resealable plastic food storage bag; add tofu. Marinate 20 to 30 minutes. Drain tofu, reserving marinade. Stir marinade into cornstarch until smooth.

2. Heat oil in large nonstick skillet or wok over medium-high heat. Add vegetables; stir-fry 2 to 3 minutes or until vegetables are crisp-tender. Add tofu; stir-fry 1 minute. Stir reserved marinade mixture; add to skillet. Bring to a boil; boil 1 minute. Serve over vermicelli.   *Makes 2 servings*

Nutrients per Serving: *Calories: 305, Calories from Fat: 20%, Total Fat: 7 g, Saturated Fat: 1 g, Protein: 19 g, Carbohydrate: 42 g, Cholesterol: 0 mg, Sodium: 824 mg, Dietary Fiber: 6 g*

Dietary Exchanges: *2 Vegetable, 2 Starch, 1 Lean Meat, 1 Fat*

Recipe Tip

To drain tofu, place it in a colander and let it stand for 5 minutes, then place it on several layers of paper towels. If extra-firm tofu is not available, use firm tofu; drain as directed above, cover with paper towels and place a small heavy plate on top. Let stand for 5 or 10 minutes, then cut into cubes.

Delicious Desserts

You'll love these easy-to-prepare low-sugar desserts.

Baked Pear Dessert

2 tablespoons dried cranberries or raisins
1 tablespoon toasted sliced almonds
⅛ teaspoon cinnamon
⅓ cup unsweetened apple cider or apple juice, divided
1 medium (6 ounces) unpeeled pear, cut in half lengthwise and cored
½ cup vanilla sugar-free low-fat ice cream

1. Preheat oven to 350°F. Combine cranberries, almonds, cinnamon and 1 teaspoon cider in bowl.

2. Place pear halves, cut side up, in small baking dish. Mound almond mixture on top of pear halves. Pour remaining cider into dish. Cover with foil.

3. Bake pear halves 35 to 40 minutes or until pears are soft, spooning cider in dish over pears once or twice during baking. Serve warm and top with ice cream.   *Makes 2 servings*

Nutrients per Serving: *Calories: 87, Calories from Fat: 19%, Total Fat: 2 g, Saturated Fat: <1 g, Protein: 1 g, Carbohydrate: 16 g, Cholesterol: 3 mg, Sodium: 13 mg, Dietary Fiber: 1 g*

Dietary Exchanges: *1 Fruit, ½ Fat*

1½ tablespoons
    gingersnap
    crumbs
    (2 snaps)
¼ teaspoon ground
    ginger
2 ounces reduced-
    fat cream
    cheese,
    softened
1 container
    (6 ounces)
    peach sugar-
    free, nonfat
    yogurt
¼ teaspoon vanilla
⅓ cup chopped fresh
    peach or
    drained canned
    peaches in juice

Peaches & Cream Gingersnap Cups

1. Combine gingersnap crumbs and ginger in small bowl; set aside.

2. Beat cream cheese in small bowl at medium speed of electric mixer until smooth. Add yogurt and vanilla. Beat at low speed until smooth and well blended. Stir in chopped peach.

3. Divide peach mixture between two 6-ounce custard cups. Cover and refrigerate 1 hour. Top each serving with half of gingersnap crumb mixture just before serving.   *Makes 2 servings*

Note: Instead of crushing the gingersnaps, serve them whole with the peaches & cream cups.

Nutrients per Serving: *Calories: 148, Calories from Fat: 34%, Total Fat: 5 g, Saturated Fat: 3 g, Protein: 6 g, Carbohydrate: 18 g, Cholesterol: 16 mg, Sodium: 204 mg, Dietary Fiber: 1 g*

Dietary Exchanges: *1 Starch, ½ Milk, 1 Fat*

1 packet sugar
substitute or
equivalent of
2 teaspoons
sugar
⅛ teaspoon ground
cinnamon
1 (6-inch) fat-free
flour tortilla
Nonstick cooking
spray
1 tablespoon
reduced-fat soft
cream cheese
⅓ cup fresh
strawberry
slices

DELICIOUS DESSERTS

Cinnamon Tortilla with Cream Cheese & Strawberries

1. Combine sugar substitute and cinnamon in cup; mix well. Heat large nonstick skillet over medium heat.

2. Lightly spray one side of tortilla with cooking spray; sprinkle with cinnamon mixture.

3. Place tortilla, cinnamon side down, in hot skillet. Cook 2 minutes or until lightly browned. Remove from skillet.

4. Spread uncooked side of tortilla with cream cheese; arrange strawberries down center of tortilla. Roll up tortilla or fold to serve.   *Makes 1 serving*

Recipe Tip: Prepare recipe through step 3. Mash a few of the strawberry slices with a fork until almost smooth; stir into cream cheese. Proceed as directed in step 4.

Nutrients per Serving: *Calories: 114, Calories from Fat: 21%, Total Fat: 3 g, Saturated Fat: 2 g, Protein: 5 g, Carbohydrate: 18 g, Cholesterol: 8 mg, Sodium: 256 mg, Dietary Fiber: 7 g*

Dietary Exchanges: *½ Fruit, 1 Starch, ½ Fat*

Recipe Tip
Use spreadable soft cream cheese for this recipe.
Look for it in 8-ounce plastic containers
in the dairy case.

Mango Vanilla Parfait

1. Prepare pudding according to package instructions using 1¼ cups milk.

2. In parfait glass or small glass bowl, layer quarter of pudding, half of mango, half of strawberries and quarter of pudding. Repeat layers in second parfait glass. Refrigerate 30 minutes.

3. Just before serving, top with cookie crumbs and garnish with strawberries.

Makes 2 servings

Nutrients per Serving: *Calories: 153, Calories from Fat: 9%, Total Fat: 1 g, Saturated Fat: 1 g, Protein: 6 g, Carbohydrate: 29 g, Cholesterol: 3 mg, Sodium: 129 mg, Dietary Fiber: 2 g*

Dietary Exchanges: *2 Starch, ½ Milk*

Recipe Tip

It you haven't tried fresh mango, you have a treat in store when you taste this lush tropical fruit. Look for fruit that is firm but not hard. Let them ripen in a paper bag at room temperature until they yield slightly to pressure and have a heavenly fragrance.

½ (4-serving size) package vanilla sugar-free instant pudding mix

1¼ cups fat-free (skim) milk

½ cup fresh mango cubes

2 large strawberries, sliced

3 sugar-free shortbread cookies, crumbled *or* 2 tablespoons reduced-fat granola

Strawberry slices for garnish

Easy Citrus Berry Shortcake

1 individual sponge
  cake
1 tablespoon
  orange juice
¼ cup lemon chiffon
  sugar-free,
  nonfat yogurt
¼ cup thawed
  frozen fat-free
  nondairy
  whipped
  topping
⅔ cup sliced
  strawberries or
  raspberries
Mint leaves
  (optional)

1. Place individual sponge cake on serving plate. Drizzle with orange juice.

2. Fold together yogurt and whipped topping. Spoon half of mixture onto cake. Top with berries and remaining yogurt mixture. Garnish with mint leaves. *Makes 1 serving*

Nutrients per Serving: *Calories: 173, Calories from Fat: 7%, Total Fat: 1 g, Saturated Fat: <1 g, Protein: 4 g, Carbohydrate: 37 g, Cholesterol: 39 mg, Sodium: 116 mg, Dietary Fiber: 3 g*

Dietary Exchanges: *1 Fruit, 1½ Starch*

½ cup peeled fresh
peach or
nectarine, cut
into chunks
1 can (5 ounces)
evaporated
skimmed milk*
¼ cup cholesterol-
free egg
substitute
1 packet sugar
substitute or
equivalent of
2 teaspoons
sugar
½ teaspoon vanilla
Cinnamon

*If a 5-ounce can is not
available, use ½ cup plus
2 tablespoons evaporated
skimmed milk.

Peach Custard

*1.*Preheat oven to 325°F. Divide peach chunks
between two 6-ounce ovenproof custard cups. Whisk
together milk, egg substitute, sugar substitute and
vanilla. Pour mixture over peach chunks in custard
cups.

*2.*Place custard cups in shallow 1-quart casserole.
Carefully pour hot water into casserole to depth of
1-inch. Bake custards 50 minutes or until knife
inserted in center comes out clean. Remove custard
cups from water bath. Serve warm or at room
temperature; sprinkle with cinnamon.

Makes 2 servings

Note: Drained canned peach slices in juice may be
substituted for fresh fruit.

Nutrients per Serving: *Calories: 52, Calories from Fat: 2%,
Total Fat: <1 g, Saturated Fat: <1 g, Protein: 5 g, Carbohydrate: 7g,
Cholesterol: <1 mg, Sodium: 71 mg, Dietary Fiber: 1 g*

Dietary Exchanges: *1 Fruit*

Recipe Tip

Since about half the water is removed from fat-free
milk to produce evaporated skimmed milk, it has
more flavor than fresh milk. If you don't like the
slightly caramelized flavor of canned milk in
a recipe, substitute fresh fat-free milk.

Cinnamon Compote

½ cup unsweetened
pineapple juice
⅛ teaspoon ground
cinnamon
1½ cups cubed
cantaloupe
½ cup blueberries

1. In small saucepan combine juice and cinnamon. Cook and stir over low heat 4 to 5 minutes or until slightly syrupy. Cool slightly.

2. Combine cantaloupe and blueberries. Pour juice mixture over fruit; toss. Refrigerate until cold.

Makes 2 servings

Nutrients per Serving: *Calories: 98, Calories from Fat: 4%, Total Fat: 1 g, Saturated Fat: <1 g, Protein: 2 g, Carbohydrate: 24 g, Cholesterol: 0 mg, Sodium: 14 mg, Dietary Fiber: 2 g*

Dietary Exchanges: *1½ Fruit*

Recipe Tip

This recipe is an easy way to dress up summer fruit, such as vitamin A-rich cantaloupe.

½ cup fresh
   blueberries
2 tablespoons all-
   purpose flour
1½ tablespoons
   granulated
   sugar
⅛ teaspoon salt
¼ teaspoon ground
   cardamom
¼ cup cholesterol-
   free egg
   substitute
1 teaspoon grated
   lemon peel
½ teaspoon vanilla
¾ cup reduced-fat
   (2%) milk
1 teaspoon
   powdered sugar

Blueberry Custard Supreme

1. Preheat oven to 350°F. Spray 1-quart soufflé or casserole dish with nonstick cooking spray. Distribute blueberries over bottom of prepared dish.

2. Whisk flour, granulated sugar, salt and cardamom in small bowl. Add egg substitute, lemon peel and vanilla; whisk until smooth and well blended. Whisk in milk. Pour over blueberries.

3. Bake 30 minutes or until puffed, lightly browned and center is set. Cool on wire rack. Serve warm or at room temperature. Sprinkle with powdered sugar just before serving.   *Makes 2 servings*

Blackberry Custard Supreme: Substitute fresh blackberries for blueberries; proceed as directed.

Nutrients per Serving: *Calories: 155, Calories from Fat: 11%, Total Fat: 2 g, Saturated Fat: 1 g, Protein: 7 g, Carbohydrate: 27g, Cholesterol: 7 mg, Sodium: 249 mg, Dietary Fiber: 1 g*

Dietary Exchanges: *½ Fruit, 1 Starch, ½ Milk*

½ cup day-old
  French bread
  cubes
1 tablespoon dried
  cranberries or
  tart cherries
⅓ cup fat-free (skim)
  milk
1 tablespoon
  refrigerated
  cholesterol-free
  egg substitute
1 tablespoon brown
  sugar
¼ teaspoon vanilla
⅛ teaspoon ground
  cinnamon

Cranberry Bread Pudding

1. Preheat oven to 350°F. Toss together bread cubes and cranberries. Place in 6-ounce custard cup.

2. Stir together milk, egg substitute, brown sugar, vanilla and cinnamon. Pour over bread mixture. Bake 22 to 25 minutes or until knife inserted in center comes out clean. Cool slightly.   *Makes 1 serving*

Nutrients per Serving: *Calories: 163, Calories from Fat: 5%, Total Fat: 1 g, Saturated Fat: <1 g, Protein: 6 g, Carbohydrate: 33 g, Cholesterol: 1 mg, Sodium: 151 mg, Dietary Fiber: 1 g*

Dietary Exchanges: *1½ Starch, ½ Milk*

Recipe Tip

Since cranberries are very tart, a little granulated sugar is added to them during processing. Dried tart cherries are not sweetened and are a good substitute for dried cranberries. However, dried tart cherries are not readily available. If they are not available in your supermarket, look for them in gourmet food stores or catalogues.

Index